HOLIDAY FROM THE PERFECT CRIME

other books by the author

POETRY
Dawn Visions
Burnt Heart/Ode to the War Dead
This Body of Black Light Gone Through the Diamond
The Desert is the Only Way Out
The Chronicles of Akhira
The Blind Beekeeper
Mars & Beyond
Laughing Buddha Weeping Sufi
Salt Prayers
Ramadan Sonnets
Psalms for the Brokenhearted
I Imagine a Lion
Coattails of the Saint
Abdallah Jones and the Disappearing-Dust Caper
Love is a Letter Burning in a High Wind
The Flame of Transformation Turns to Light
Underwater Galaxies
The Music Space
Cooked Oranges
Through Rose Colored Glasses
Like When You Wave at a Train and the Train Hoots Back at You
In the Realm of Neither
The Fire Eater's Lunchbreak
Millennial Prognostications
You Open a Door and it's a Starry Night
Where Death Goes
Shaking the Quicksilver Pool
The Perfect Orchestra
Sparrow on the Prophet's Tomb
A Maddening Disregard for the Passage of Time
Stretched Out on Amethysts
Invention of the Wheel
Sparks Off the Main Strike
Chants for the Beauty Feast
In Constant Incandescence
Holiday from the Perfect Crime

THEATER / THE FLOATING LOTUS MAGIC OPERA COMPANY
The Walls Are Running Blood
Bliss Apocalypse

PROSE
Zen Rock Gardening
The Little Book of Zen
Zen Wisdom

HOLIDAY FROM THE PERFECT CRIME

POEMS

JANUARY 25 — JUNE 11, 2005

Daniel Abdal-Hayy Moore

The Ecstatic Exchange
2011
Philadelphia

Holiday from the Perfect Crime
Copyright © 2011 Daniel Abdal-Hayy Moore
All rights reserved.
Printed in the United States of America

For quotes any longer than those for critical articles and reviews, contact:
The Ecstatic Exchange,
6470 Morris Park Road, Philadelphia, PA 19151-2403
email: abdalhayy@danielmoorepoetry.com

First Edition
ISBN: 978-0-578-08293-6 (paper)
Published by *The Ecstatic Exchange*,
6470 Morris Park Road, Philadelphia, PA 19151-2403

Also available from The Ecstatic Exchange:
Knocking from Inside, poems by Tiel Aisha Ansari

Cover collage by the author
Back cover photograph by Peter Sanders
Text set in Garamond Adobe and Premier Pro by the author, based on styles created by Ian Whiteman, master designer & calligrapher

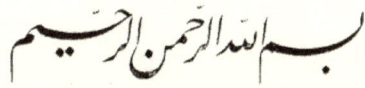

DEDICATION

To
Shaykh ibn al-Habib
(and the continuation of the Habibiyya)
Shaykh Bawa Muhaiyuddeen,
all shuyukh of instruction and ma'arifa,
to the beloved memory of
Marco Antonio Montes de Oca
and Eugene Gonder,
and to
Baji Tayyaba Khanum
of the unsounded depths

The earth is not bereft
of Light

CONTENTS

Author's Foreword   9
Where Feet are Superfluous   11
First and Last Lion   13
Savage and Silly   15
A Line All by Itself   16
Hotel Delirium   17
The Glimpse   19
The Sin of the Shoe   21
Stauffer Makes a Long Landing   23
To Maintain the Proper Temperature   25
On the Lip of Sleep   27
The Bullet   29
The Narrative   32
The Blues   35
The Surgeon   36
Giant Steps   38
Silence Overtakes Us in the End   39
Zog The Speechless Anthracite   42
The Wild Red Rooster   43
Trilogy   45
One Line Poem / "One day..."   48
Lines Written During a Flu   49
The Boy Who Sought to Put Death to Death   50
One Line Poem / "The cat..."   53
Takeeti Tapeeti   54
Flying Saucers   57
The Key Motivation   59
Each   61
The Non-Existent Noble Arch   63
Line Left Over From a Dream   66

The Sumptuous Honey of Words   67
The Lover The Beloved   69
It Should Be Enough   71
On Reading a New Poem by Jack Gilbert   73
Facts Can Be Broken But the Truth Remains   75
I Went Down to the Diner   78
Ghost Poem   82
Shellac   83
The Dolphin Chorus   85
Couplets (Punjabi Style)   88
One Line Poem / "Life..."   91
Mercury Pond   92
The Forty-Four Emerald Earrings of Madame Chang   94
The Matter at Hand   96
Late-Night Lexicons   98
Ten Thousand Buffalo   99
Love's Pebbles Thrown   101
Death Drove a Red Potato   104
Those Rose Bushes Out Back   107
Slaphappy   109
In Sleep   111
Sophocles Upon a Lowly Promontory   112
Sandwiched in Between Two Universes   114
Poetics   117
Poem for Robert Desnos   118
Enigmatic Poem for My Mother   119
To Suppose That We'll Live Forever   121
Five Short Meditations on the Virgin Mary   122
Holiday from the Perfect Crime   128

Index   132

AUTHOR'S FOREWORD

Perhaps I have no reason to defend some of the titles of my books of poetry, *Cooked Oranges, Stretched Out on Amethysts, A Maddening Disregard for the Passage of Time*, etc. They are, as Popeye said, what they are, and in a way are compressed one-line poems on their own, with often only a kind of kissing relationship to the poems inside.

So now *Holiday from the Perfect Crime*, as the majority of all of my titles do, came to me at the outset between books, and stuck throughout the writing of the poems found here. Perhaps I was watching too many crime shows on TV, or responding to my wife Malika's half-earnest urging for me to "write a best-seller." (How envious we writers and poets often are of the hard-bitten crime novelists, the Damon Runyons and Dashiell Hammetts of the world, even as we try to elevate our works to a spiritual plane, but one that crackles and is as crisp as the best crime dialog.)

But that isn't what's operative here. Somehow the resonance for me during the soft humming of this title as an abiding albeit background theme for the poems, was the perfect crime of our existence: perfect because created by a Perfect Creator. A crime because we get up to such malfeasance at the lower end of it, and a crime at the higher end in the sense that the Sufis and other mystics often mention, that any existence of ours before Allah *ta'ala*, any flake or residue of our self-ness, tawdry or fine, is a crime, a flaw, a fluttering obstruction before the strong, essential Light of God. This, of course, is at the extreme height of spiritual elevation, and perhaps not for everyone to realize nor even understand, nor can I say I myself have reached that place, but do envision it. But when you have met and sat with a saint (*wali, a friend of God*) of whatever divinely revealed practice, you do get the sense of a personality honed to its finest hair-thin, feather-light "membrane," and even that virtually vanished, before the Divine Consciousness. These are men and women whose actions and words and thoughts are soaked in light to such a degree that the person is human in essential-most radiance, by being effaced before God in His greater, ever-present and infinitely Merciful manifestations or self-revealings in the world. Such people exist among us on this earth, have always and always will until the Last Days, and we benefit in untold ways by their presence, either known or unbeknownst to us. Each of their gestures is a teaching — they elevate us with just a glance even before a word is spoken. They are what prophetic "religions" are really all about, and they transmit it to us to enter into those domains ourselves, thus "solving" the perfect crime by "dissolving" or at least reducing the dangerousness of the criminal ego and its self-interested intents.

So what, then, would constitute a *holiday* from that "perfect crime?" The opposite of perfection? A libertine vacation from such rigorous consciousness? But the word "holiday" comes from Old English *hāligdæg*, Holy Day, so a holy day from that state would be an epiphany, a release from "criminal taint" into illumination.

I have always felt that the purpose and intent of true poetry is illumination, for oneself and others, in its details and in its vision, in the Bodhissatvic sense of everyone entering Nirvana before we do, that we might all bathe in the Presence of Allah in creation where *"everywhere you turn, there is the Face of Allah."* So the poems in this book may not completely "personify" the title, but as an abiding sub-theme, I dearly hope its incense at least smokes through them and makes them sweet.

Nihil potest homo intelligere sine phantasmate
Man cannot know anything without images

— *Saint Thomas Aquinas*

GOD

The essence of his method
is to be present
everywhere

— *Katalin Mezey*

... stallions were prancing
in their places, like letters of the alphabet.

— *Osip Mandelstam*

WHERE FEET ARE SUPERFLUOUS

I searched everywhere for the perfect escape
now that the giant lobsters were closing in

I disguised myself briefly as a piece of kelp
and they scuttled by with red claws waving
eye-feelers waggling

I changed my profession and became a rookie shoe salesman
just like my first High School job in downtown Oakland

Zebras were the hardest to shoe
especially if they stood in front of zigzag black & white drapery

Shoes are the underclass of the world
they serve and are thrown out when worn out

Laceable or laceless they look forward wherever we go
and though they might be tempted they never
treat us like heels

They toe the line and are always in step
and if they have tongues they keep them to themselves

The more we trod on them the more soft-hearted
they become

If they can fit our feet why can't we fit the
world as snugly?

Some places people go shoeless and they are
brave and casual and won't get pinched
where they stand

They feel the earth's energies coming up through their feet
direct and it makes them go lightly

Angels don't wear shoes unless perhaps they're
impersonating someone in more formal attire

They go on their rounds in various stages of elevation
and the ground is really beneath them

God doesn't need shoes though one of His
most devoted servants at the time of Moses
used to proclaim endearments by suggesting
he would dust them and care for them
especially well

I thought of disguising myself as a pair of shoes
and walking away from the whole thing
leave the world behind while still in it

But I must have not wanted it enough for
like Newton I walk on the earth with gravity

glad to God I still put one foot in front of the other
till the day of my death when shoeless I'll go
also gladly to where even feet are superfluous

FIRST AND LAST LION

The last lion leaves its mane and its great
cat face emerges without its majestic
halo of hair

He is also the first
the first lion to enter the thicket of banyan trees
seeking his sustenance in the interstices between
shadows

He rolls in the first and last sunlight like a
rainbow coiled around a hole
shedding radiant rings

Earths sumptuous with rich vegetation flow through his
form from void formlessness on his dark side
to the delicate shapes of beauty nutritious on
this side our side the

side from which we witness him in leonine
comprehension

Give him fire and he'll stride right through

Give him utter darkness and his roar will pierce
the silence like a clock

Many elephants fit inside him such is his girth
many earths fit inside his elegance in free-floating
space

He's left the mane of his halo like a galaxy in its
particular nimbus suspended in motion in space

But if you encounter him say hello and
invite him for tea

Inner flowering is never far from his beauty

His span is eternity

1/26

SAVAGE AND SILLY

Savage and silly by turns the poem puts on
a pair of silver shoes (the ones with

little fluttering wings at the ankles) to take us
on a guided tour of the thickest forest and the
most exotic medicinal plants and half-asleep
or wide-awake creatures uncurling from their
lairs at this strange hour for visiting

But the poem while respectful due to its
loyalty to syntax however wrenched or displaced
also looks with naked eyes

at the newborn zebra bursting from its egg
or a seed case busting open
to produce a living flame

1/29

A LINE ALL BY ITSELF

The maximum sentence for all of us is life

HOTEL DELIRIUM

At Hotel Delirium the guests never sleep
some at the excitement of being alive
others at the thought of death that hammers their minds

The fish ponds at Hotel Delirium are full of croaking koi
and frogs that remain silent even at night

The moon reflects in the Hotel Delirium pond
but the surface shimmers and shimmies constantly

At Hotel Delirium there's no need for wallpaper
the white blank walls are screens for the most
appalling and enthralling hallucinations

Some see God among the branches or pausing by the lake
others are terrified by the spiny and aggressive imps they see
propelling forward into their living space

Hotel Delirium is always booked day and night every
day or night of the year
yet uncannily there's always room for more and
more always come

Hotel Delirium sits on a haunted hill and tilts at an angle
or rather many angles its gables and turrets and of course
the owls and ravens that abound on its parapets

But Hotel Delirium also abides in sun-flooded kitchens
in rainbow-hued interiors with all the latest gadgets

There's never been a bomb threat at Hotel Delirium
in fact those who would threaten have a suite
all to themselves

If you wake up at Hotel Delirium one fine day
wake up again
the horses outside the window are not on fire
and the trees are not torches

A Continental Breakfast is served at Hotel Delirium
not for the faint hearted
comprised of world headlines baked in a pie

Checkout time is any time at Hotel Delirium
Take your stuffed fish and your violins and the
others of your clan

No one stays forever at Hotel Delirium although
it's so much nicer to leave on your own two feet

2/1

THE GLIMPSE

The silken snow of earth is nothing compared to
the silkiness of snow beyond this earth

Though for all that we always rely on earthly
equivalents as I just did

Space in the next world is nothing like space in this

Items there are like items here in suddenly
sharp focus as if everything here is a
fuzzy picture in dire need of focus

Each water drop ascending in its upward arc of a
fountain taking its sweet time and being then
part of a crystalline display there beyond this
earth we can only allude to as being a

giant diamond brooch or chandelier of the
beauteous glints in your eyes or a
fireworks of stars against a black night so
visible each spark is a new conflagration

And to walk there on snow is beyond crunching

And the whiteness there is beyond being blindingly so

And the stretch in all rolling directions at once
since there's no "direction" as such there

is a pure instance of spatial ecstasy

or the way a horizon cuts sky from earth here

there is only superb continuity immediately
seen by the eye or the heart's eye
also indivisibly joyous so all we can do is
praise the Giver and Displayer and Originator

of that which is so far beyond our capacity of
description but even this gift's given to us

that often our envisioning itself exceeds our grasp
and what is here is only a pointer and a proof
for those of us who may need no proof but are

grateful for a glimpse
however furtive

2/3

THE SIN OF THE SHOE

It's a sin to wear one shoe and set the
other shoe on fire

It's a sin to put your mother and all her
children including you in a shoe and then
put your foot in it and walk on it

that's a sin

It's a sin to cut down a tree and put it
in the shoe and set it adrift and then walk along
in only one shoe

It's a sin to stuff your shoe full of holy books
then stuff your foot in it and start dancing

It's a sin to kick with one shoe while the
other shoe is chatting politely with a pair of high heels

that's a sin

It's a sin to invite other feet to join you for
drinks in your shoe and then put it on

It's a sin to write *"I love you"* in your
shoe and then to tread on it with
smelly feet

It's a sin to wait forever for the other

shoe to drop and then cut off the whole leg
and drop it instead

If you polish one shoe you must polish both

If you lace one shoe but leave the other unlaced
that's a sin

If you hope the shoe will walk by itself without you
that's not a sin that's a fantasy

Don't expect your shoe to come between you and
the earth

The earth is also a kind of shoe which must be
treated with respect

If you scuffle with your shoe where no
scuffling is allowed you better be a
good scuffler or it's a sin

Don't let one shoe know what the
other is doing

If the shoe fits
wear it

STAUFFER MAKES A LONG LANDING

Heliotrope helicopters of light scatter
radiance in all directions until even the

walls become transparent and we walk through them
transparency past transparency into
cloudless climes and rocky outcroppings over

nothingness that doesn't actually exist since
He's put life into every niche and cranny every

gnat gnashes its teeth every spark conflagrates throughout in
ubiquitous showerings of brightness as if the
entire universe with its chiaroscuro of galaxies some in
rosy explosions others in gold or silver halos

were folded very small and then shot through again with
the light of supreme transcendence more
dazzling than a direct light bulb more

in harmony with the perfect darkness of God's
acceptance in satisfaction of our satisfied souls
than endless black velvet stretching from
end to end

from one end to the other

The unfathomable total darkness of
His love the depth of which

no heart however lit with
shattering canyons of crystalline light

can plumb

2/5

(Note: the title came to me from dream upon waking, while the poem came separately, and I have no idea who Stauffer is, perhaps the helicopter pilots of the first line, or why he's made a "long landing," but perhaps that's the poem itself?)

TO MAINTAIN THE PROPER TEMPERATURE

To maintain the proper temperature at all times
by driving back and forth through the door cut
in the giant sequoia in forest darkness under the canopy
you must breathe in gentle bursts and your
heartbeat coincide with tides and the
growth of roses

Don't think the accidental hasn't been already
figured in to the outcome
each filament hair perfectly in place and each
mustache firmly drawn across the Mona Lisa

To maintain our stance vis-à-vis the cyclotronic
passage of time for example
is not exactly a laughing matter though some
laughter may take a few seconds while some
like the last laugh by he who laughs best may
go on for millennia

Spot the green horse in the grassy hillside
and you'll win a garden gate and two
gate posts where there's neither this side nor
that to either contain or exclude with fence or
passageway

We've all been invited to the final celebration
so bring your first impression and your lasting memory
with no expectations and all will be well
though the soap may get away between the

chandeliers before the light can clean up all the
darkness in such thick abundance here

You've bet on being found out before you're
forced to confess
it's a noble strategy though full confessions are
seldom admitted and many a crime goes for ages
unsolved and unrequited

Self-knowledge is like a pencil writing itself
or a clock looking itself in the face
it can't be frozen in time and space for
all time and all space

Nothing stays the same long enough and
the incessant winds bring new
messages constantly into the mix

The echo that you hear is the one voice of everything
giving the semblance of multiplicity
a thousand white horses are spilling out of its timbre
a thousand black shadows are cast on its tonal
slide

The night is coming faster than we expected
but we're ready for it with flashlight and
compass to point us toward true Mecca every time

2/9

ON THE LIP OF SLEEP

On the lip of sleep
on the runway of waking up where I've just
taxied to a stop

everything is pretty much where I left it
though I could be elsewhere for all I know
having come out from a full life of dream

to collect bottles in Mongolia
or farm a few acres of rice paddy in Bali

There was such involvement in the dream I
just had though now I can't remember what or
why

This side I have to get up to pee with
lamp light showing the room as I left it
pretty much the way it was as far as I know
though if I opened every book and it was
Sanskrit I'd be convinced otherwise

This side has the semblance of reality
but at this juncture this fine edge
tissue-paper thin though seemingly
solid as an ox
can't be relied on

The bedside travel clock ticks the way a
cat purrs

The purring cat sits facing her direction the way a clock sits

There's a high hum

but am I home?

2/10

THE BULLET

The bullet sped through the air
going nowhere

Aunt Martha was ironing
ironically enough

On a high balcony
in Barcelona

Larvae take a few hours or days
to mature and then
look out!

The clothes were neatly pressed in a pile
and then piled in a press

Time has a way of keeping still
for important events

Nothing greases silence better
than an important event

Time was winding down
and space was sharpening to a point

Travel from A to B is often sudden
and brutal

A direct consequence of a true

concatenation of events

poising a conclusion on the
head of a pin

which punctures the silence
with a bang

heard round the world
from balcony to bridge to battleship to
bathysphere bobbing in the bath of life

The bullet sped forward and
didn't look back

With grim determination
it didn't know where it was going

Though where it landed was the
end of all knowledge itself

As many waves as crest on the open sea
or clouds in the scudding sky

or something whistling through the wind
to deliver destiny's personal blow

like a signed love letter dipped in scent
and sent through the perfume of the air
to a fair beloved

Though we don't know it each blow is a
love blow

The children were playing on the terrace
hoops and jacks and hopscotch and Clue

The president was signing documents at his desk
flags of all nations furled and unfurled
behind him

Like a kiss it landed where it
needed to land

Sent from a serious hand

The young soldier in mid-sentence
put a period to his life sentence

Though he never finished his last sentence
sentenced to eternal transcendence

Aunt Martha ironed another shirt
he'd wear only once

on a balcony in Barcelona

On a hilltop overlooking the sea

On a day without clouds

Above the noisy city

2/12

THE NARRATIVE

"I have a narrative to tell you" says the
criminal to his crime

And the policeman who apprehends him

And the policeman's mother on her knees

And her grandfather as he stops the lathe

And his father standing by the blown-down shack

And his grandfather who stood up in the assembly

And the old woman who was his mother one day
in steerage

Each one tells a part of the narrative the part they
know or think they know of what
happened to them or they think happened to them

to the orchestral sound of their voice with its
crescendos and diminuendos

The narrative of the wheel of fire that broke through the
wall of their bedroom and the uphill march of
shadows across that wall before it happened

The narrative of the forest cries not by owls or men
as the dawn comes up and they feel the earth

revolve beneath them

The story of the darkness becoming personified
and hearing its voice for the first time

God tapped it once and it shivered and became light
when no one was around and that was the
story

The first touch that set it in motion with its
verbs and consonants in order and its
descriptions and sensations set into words

A small fly buzzes across that can't
wait to tell its story to the

first fly it sees

"It all began the day I stole my first watch"
says the criminal to his crime

The policeman says he was caught once with another's money
and was determined to stop crime once and for all

Whose mother saw her uncle slap his wife

And her grandfather shot a man in the war
who wouldn't die

And his father saved all his money for passage to come here

Whose grandfather dared to defy the governors
in front of the whole town and ended in jail

As predicted by the mother in steerage as she
took her son in her arms and told a story about

the new world they'd discover together
without wheels of fire or shadows on walls
or cries in the night

just before dawn

2/14

THE BLUES

There's a funny dark road between my toes
and a snail on fire
it can't light the way like a Chinese lantern
though its flames flare up from its spiraling back
like a wheel

If the forest is dark and the light between my
eyes doesn't light the way what'll I do?

If the night is a square box around me
and the forest can just be glimpsed through its
transparent sides with its paths and its
wolverines how can I proceed?

There's a bandage wound round my head in a
spiral and a landscape in the bandage of a
forest of flaming trees

This is a blues though it's full of blacks and flickering reds
and no sure way home

Dear God blast through the box and take me to my
heart!

2/17

THE SURGEON

A surgeon must have keen eyesight *sangfroid*
and a steady hand

under which a living organism lies comatose and
full of hope as it slid into sleep that it will
wake up transformed into a swan or

fiery phoenix lying in its own ashes hitting the
ceiling with its head

The surgeon puts out his hands
gets new gloves looks down onto another patient
who's a few paces away from death already
jutting over grave's edge under the overhead light

Angels have begun crowding the room
sound has gotten thinner and higher
memories have become strained and
essentialized to a few majors like
being born and the near-death experience 50 years ago at the
Grand Canyon 4:15 in the afternoon with
bright sunlight and extra-long shadows
wrapped in a golden gauze

The surgeon's hands are like horses grazing on new grass
like cascades of deep forest water never before witnessed
by the eyes of man
or the turning key in a steamer trunk forgotten in an
attic in Connecticut back in 1895

and out fly a thousand white moths
heading for the window

When the patient wakes up not dead she
looks out the window

The surgeon's already asleep in the middle of a
railroad dream in the Alps with his wife
driving the kids to school

The various patients who didn't survive
are photographs in a ledger and
names on a list

Angels appear in other rooms to other sleepers
like bright sunlight flashing out of dark clouds

on steep Alpine slopes

                                                                            2/18

GIANT STEPS

Take giant steps and giants will come
down from their Teutonic mountains or wherever
they dwell at the time and lift you over the

door ledge that stands in the Himalayas or
wherever the highest peak is to lead you
across the cloud expanse with your
feet firmly planted in fresh fields of

clover or whatever vegetation surrounds the
journeying feet of a pilgrim whose goal is
emblazoned like a mirror lodged in the heart
for the corresponding mirror image that will
achieve it with a flash burst of light of

reflection meeting reflection so the whole
practitioner disappears and only a high
sailing note like a piccolo remains both
glorifying the disincarnate Lord and

being in fact the very note played by His own lips

heard once in the air
surrounded by a clapping of wings

2/21

SILENCE OVERTAKES US IN THE END

for Andrei Ciortan

God may not always be in the forefront
of every event or conversation

Trucks rumble past horses gallop or the room jolts
or just stands still

A hush lands over everything like bed sheets over
furniture in mountain cabins for the winter

A married couple after years together becomes *incommunicado*
and impulses that start in the heart die in the

embryonic stage

But in the molecules a lantern's lit
and already wobbling in the dark to

show the road

Even Galapagos reptiles blinkless gaze with their
black eyes at sun and moon

In deepest canyons water drips or roars

And you there on your bicycle riding an icicle

I cannot contain enough of the world

yet I contain it all

A cataract inside and inside that cataract
calm

Could we see God in the clouds if the
clouds move aside?

I've answered a thousand questions already
without moving a single tongue

Yet the fact remains God might not occur to us
if God didn't let us know

Not the man in the Chinese herb shop with the whiskers
smoking punk

Original shadows cast by original stones

Cries over canyons by that one bird that
makes that cry

Scrolls are inky with His Attributes
but a mouse knows them already creeping

through fields of grain

Is the secret rolled under ocean rolls and
heaved with its heaves?

The thief knows it the minute he becomes a thief

that negative theologian of things

It's Colonel Mustard in the Study with the Wrench

Silence overtakes us in the end

2/22

ZOG THE SPEECHLESS ANTHRACITE

Zog the speechless anthracite spoke first:

*"If we should find you we would hide you
somewhere under our tongues*

*If we should lose you we would blind you
for we are ruthless rogues"*

So we ran from the world and hid in this heart
whose beats are like rain on a windowpane

under a tall mountain

2/25

THE WILD RED ROOSTER

The wild red rooster crows at dawn
and motes and mites scurry to get in formation
atoms and chromosome-rows invisible to the
eye but capable of the most astounding feats

Silence follows with its blank banners and its
ocean surf suddenly stopped in its tracks
but for just such a small increment that
neither any body nor any thing notices

That's when golden light occurs in a hidden window

That's when lips form new words and old
languages shade into darkness verb by verb
and nouns take one last look at the creation they
so happily named before heading down into oblivion forever
for a spot of space and time so quick nothing
flying stops its flight and nothing
thought stops its curious linkage

The entire universe lies unnamed by any tongue
as nakedly itself and speechless as nothing imaginable
and this poem can't even continue past that
subatomically microscopic abyss without
holding its breath

Then a wave waves air airs light lights
and love loves in circulatory crannies
God's Names flowing out again like

supersonic sailboats tacking slightly with
full sails trimmed bows cutting through surf and
dolphins again leaping ahead into
unknown waters with that uncanny
delphinoid smile on their lovely
rubbery lips with that bright knowledge that

none of us lacks and none of us incontrovertibly
clicks

3/4

TRILOGY

1

I feel like a huge gray tanker going out across
black water in the blackest night with no

lights anywhere neither above in the sky or
on the horizon where the city was nor even on

board the ship braving almost arctic cold and
slosh of cold sea tumultuously crossing the bow with

scarecrow spray alone in the somber
wilderness of sky and water

2

A rat's tooth breaks the rind as much as
an angel's touch and the

pulp pours out

The world glows with an unworldly light
from near and far

It glows green inside a mason jar
on a sill of Saturnian sunlight

There's no one around to see us die

no one to see the vertical light from needle tip
to tip of sky

There's no one here at all
even as human shadows glide along a wall

Little murmuring voices keep us in thrall

toward which our ears grope hopefully

3

A bird of flame sits on her eggs
and boils them

But this is a mythical bird so the chicks hatch
like burners on a stove

Soon the sky is filled with flying flames

Their song is deeper and wilder than most bird song

They traverse the sky like a forest fire
Their great fiery plumage rivaling the sun's

When they find their mates they make a
conjoined conflagration

A brief flash almost obliterates the night

The heart is like that
inflamed by the passion of God's love

Seven seas might evaporate under the scorching heat

This is not mythological nor ontological

This is the blaze that should burn us all

Till we are a giant plumed bird
each feather ignited by remembrance of its Source

which is flight through every forest night might present us with

to light it by our torch of
unreasonable love

3/9-3/13

ONE LINE POEM

One day I'll be dead

3/15

LINES WRITTEN DURING A FLU

When we're sick we forget what it's like to be well

When we're well we forget what it's like to be ill

3/17

THE BOY WHO SOUGHT TO PUT DEATH TO DEATH

There once was an extraordinary boy
who lived through plague war and famine
and decided to go out and put death to death
once and for all

He would catch it in the act and hack it to pieces

He'd ride his horse roughshod over it and cast it in the sea
but he'd rid life of death forever so we'd be freed from it
for good

Everywhere he went in search of death he was
too late
death left shells of bodies behind always
going on ahead somewhere with no indication where it would
strike again sometimes letting the deathly ill
recover sometimes cutting down the innocent in
mid-breath or mid-heartbeat

But the boy was determined to catch death naked and
alone somehow
with no plan in mind but brute determination

A horse hobbled by and sank to its knees and died

A bird fell out of a tree

A plow sliced a snake in two
but the boy always showed up late and

death was already nowhere and everywhere
out of sight

A fire broke out in a small house but
everyone was saved

An avalanche rolled down a hillside but
the villagers were warned by the rumbling

A boat sank but everyone swam to shore

The boy was more determined than ever

things wouldn't be allowed to continue

Some babies born alive some born dead
He'd cancel death out of the equation

He stood on a tall mountain

He watched hawks dive at smaller
birds and catch them

He looked out over the valleys
smoke from chimneys curled up in the air
a funeral procession wound its way through a gorge

Where was death?
How could he trap it if he couldn't see it?
A fly landed on his knee and he
swatted it

Its crumpled body fell onto the gravel at his
feet

He wiped his hand on his pant leg
suddenly feeling sad that he'd taken even a

fly's life from it as it was going on its way

                                                      3/17

ONE LINE POEM

The cat is always so elegant in her furs

3/17

TAKEETI TAPEETI

Takeeti Tapeeti is a place you can't find
on any map

It's southwest of almost anything you can name

It's an island in an anonymous chain of islands
all of them extreme southwest of wherever you
happen to start

Looked at from above Taheeti Tapeeti is in the
shape of a large sock
though at sunset if you squint it's in the
shape of a giant rosebush

It's uninhabited except for a grandmother a
species of kangaroo no bigger than a large rat
twelve species of ant three of butterfly *(and
one of those with two heads)* and fifty-three
of birds found on none of the other islands

The water sloshes deep magenta around its
shores like a neck with its head cut off

The grandma wears a contraption of feathers
and subsists on fruits and nut meats and
is said to be over a thousand years old

The language she speaks has long-since died out
but since she's by herself and only talks to

the clouds as they pass and the animals that
stand still long enough there's no way to
know for sure though the verbs and nouns are said to be
the last repositories of pre-deluge wisdom
though it can't be very wise if it led finally
to the flood

Her face is a weather-beaten moon-mask of light
she wears palm fronds and latticework and
represents the bird spirits only of souls who
are to come not of those who've departed

and though she's by herself and very old she still
practices a kind of youth cult

The island's landscape is the most majestic
lonely and musical in the world
as the formations of coral and volcanic pumice
make giant wind flutes of all sizes and registers
so that at all hours of the day and night
eerily beautiful music can be heard woven through with
song from the fifty-three indigenous birds and the
tiny crackle from ant mandibles as the
rat-size kangaroos thump through the underbrush
in search of football size Yuyu fruit to eat

Some of the flutes are the size of giant pipe organs
and sometimes the music sounds like the most
complex polyphonic crisscross rhythms and modes of
Bach played by unseen islanders with only a
slender grasp of western notation and scales

though the wind is the ensemble and its
forceful pouring through the tubular pipes is the
only musician on the island

On some nights the grandmother dances to these lunar
tunes with her arm motions telling the
indecipherable history of Takeeti Tapeeti
for all to hear and see

though since no one's there but the aforementioned
fauna and the insensible flora

there's no way of telling what that impeccable
history really is

3/18

FLYING SAUCERS

I wonder if flying saucers or UFOs were in
shapes other than saucers they'd be more authentic

I've often thought the shape we usually think of was
dreamed up by the inventor of the Frisbee™ a few
years before launching that ubiquitous toy

But if the shape were instead say a
door in the sky that just opens with its
gangplank diagonalling down so the fleecy
cloud-creatures or the ganglia-like jelly folk could
wriggle down

Or it might be the top of a mountain on a
mountaintop and it just opens up and all the
slithering or twirling or however-propelled creatures would
sort of zigzag down the mountainsides into the
unsuspecting hamlets below

Or they might enter our world via the sea
and suddenly emerge with water sloshing from their
intricate cabs in the shapes of Tang Dynasty pagodas say
all the dragon cornices actual dragons frothing suds

Yet on the other hand they might be shaped like the
common cow or a whole herd of cows and
what was a gentle grazing afternoon is now a
riot of extraterrestrials taking off their cow-suits
and their cow jet propulsion gear having

come in the night to coincide with children's
Bedtime Story Hour for the storybook associations
for camouflage of *cow over moon*

There's something too Betty Furness in the
present image of spinning metal plate or flashing cigar

Rather an intricate ice palace affair that slowly
lights down from the sky onto an adequate
empty lot all flashing from multi-dimensional
facets with turrets and sloping esplanades and
appropriate fireworks of announcement

Turning the sky for a moment almost inside-out
so that multitudes of stars appear on
earth for a change making even the

night sky in New Mexico seem almost
twinkle-less in comparison

3/19

THE KEY MOTIVATION

The key motivation for all this
with all its peculiar

avalanches and tidal waves and houses
getting up on their piles and walking off down

hillsides to take mud baths or flashing
daggers in the dark and screams or two-headed
babies and skullduggery in the Savings & Loan Industry

God's spectacular self-revelation in little things as well as
big epiphanies of tiny noises as well as
thunderous Victoria Falls-immense lightning crashes

What's brought into the Central Chamber in a
little perfect jewel-encrusted box with silver filigree
and us given the key to open it on a glass
table bigger than Iowa

is
(when the lid is pushed back) a flood of
light not a miasma of darkness that
makes us cough uncontrollably

and what Chamber we're brought to as the
clamoring outside grows faint is not

worse tragedy but somehow the peace that
descends on a hillside of grazing cows the original

sekina of peace that comes into everything even in the
midst sometimes of the terrors themselves

and what head lifts with its eyes to look at us
is a benign head not a head of wrath

and the gaze that meets ours is topaz eyes with skies
bright with clouds and passing birds which

engulf our eyes ultimately in their own
sweet godly seeing

and at the heart of the world
a praise song

gong

3/21

EACH

On each peach an angel turns
with the progress of the sun

On each latch is full closure
or an opening

In each ditch is a hallowed hall
where echoes engender more echoings

On each porch is a lookout
across a swan-filled lake

With each scratch is relief germane
to its particular itching

With each reach is a greater arch
to allow us greater grasping

In each inch a multitude
of visionary faces

Each hatching moment
brings us new endearment

Each ache resounds like a gamelan
with its low bongs and deeper gongs

Each "h" aspirated has a
hidden "h" unsounded

He is in each
but isn't multiplied

3/23

THE NON-EXISTENT NOBLE ARCH

The non-existent noble arch that
brings us closer to true Light across the non-existent

barricades and boundaries is made of
purest non-existence so that it does in fact

exist but not in the usual way
it's collapsible portable impossible impulsive
immediate and released on a seeming whim

and answers prayers

This arch of feather-down blown into a fluff
by an arctic bellow this leap by a silver
drink from a glass chalice this that

leaves lips and ignites hearts (God's wishes)
His secret design making of this world the utter
wonderland it is with its

endless pain and instant relief from sorrow
our remembrance and our forgetfulness

Opens what was closed and for purposes of
real leaping closes what was open

Each moment takes us out of squalor
as eyelids close and open to an Amazonian paradise
with those melodious monkey-cries and cockatoo

sightings between sun rays

To the urban moment again illumined through the
twenty-thousand facets of its diamond stillness
amid the plashing of luxurious waters

Ah – it's none of this
it's in the genetic hopefulness
that accompanies us unfailingly past the
edges of the forest fire while wild
beasts leap to safety

It's in a courage we don't have and an acute
thirst we no longer cultivate and an endurance
worthy of him whose liver was plucked by an eagle

Prometheus God's first light-snatcher
strapped on the rocks as renewed daylight

Its non-existence only highlights our non-existence
before His Pure Existence once all the
theater screens and veils are dissolved with a
gull's cry and an uncurling wave on a

disappearing shore in a radiance that
doesn't originate from any created orb

up from a non-existent below and down from a
non-existent above that crisscrosses all our
existence in its gossamer web

And when we're wrapped tight in its
consumable thread

Light spreads and leaves us upright

within His purest
implacable insight

                                                         3/28

LINE LEFT OVER FROM A DREAM

You can die for love of money!

3/29

THE SUMPTUOUS HONEY OF WORDS

The sumptuous honey of words
I thought to myself but I'm not sure
after that

Drips in the heat of moonlight which isn't true but

has a strange resonance of turning nocturnal cold
upside-down as if a *house* were to

clop into view with its roof saddle askew

Or the ocean that pent-up bastion of repetition
were to get up shake itself off and go inland for a
night on the town which we've seen in
recent devastations and human sacrifice

The honey of words drips onto the wafer and is
consumed the way real honey is

A door opens and a magistrate appears in full
regalia and makes decrees

A door opens and a raggedy boy appears
with a straw hat on and a broad
smile on his face hot enough to melt *the honey of words*

In the same space rapine or rapture salvation or
loss

God's slender Presence between the two to cast
one against the other or both out the same door

It's not a linguistic subservience we live in
so much as a wordless space we fill with
thought balloons

Krakatoa's 1883 explosion blew the island itself apart
the sound of it traveled the earth twelve times around
wave after wave more horrendous than water though
perhaps less destructive outwardly

yet it may have driven the souls of those just born
whose tiny ears were shattered by it
to wage explosive tumult
back into earth's atmosphere

God in His Majestic manifestation
silencing the air
with the *sumptuous honey of words*

all clear

all clear

3/30

THE LOVER THE BELOVED

The lover lowers her gaze and the Beloved
raises it

until lover is engulfed in oceans too vast to
circumscribe

and around their margins fly continuous bands of
singing birds

The lover closes her lips around silence the way
light enters a room and obliterates darkness

and the Beloved suddenly starts singing inside the
lover's mouth until even the stars like wandering animals
in their constellational shifts bleat and bay across
vast astronomical distances making them as small

as the moisture bead on the lover's lip and the
Beloved's eye-gleam from as far away as
deep undersea

The lover stands to embrace the Beloved
and the Beloved stands to embrace the lover
and the lover stands to embrace the Beloved
and the Beloved stands to embrace the lover

and the echoes from their movements blow rainbow
lights stuttering against earth's canyon walls and icebergs

break off and slide into black water

And the Beloved stands and the lover
shrinks within the microscopic compass of all her
insignificant acts until each breath
obliterates her

and the Beloved stands to embrace the lover
until the whole world rises to a standing position
within that embrace

An ant gnaws at a redwood tree and it
falls as a straw across a single heartbeat

We've never left God's glorious dimension
and need only look
not within us nor around us
but through the sphere of that Glance the

Beloved takes and
blows into a ball of sky and crashing waves

which is all the lover offers through the paucity of
her multifaceted embrace

4/2

IT SHOULD BE ENOUGH

It should be enough and
maybe it is

but never exactly

The green coffin bobbing in a purple sea between
us and it

The many farewells or slaps in the face by
wintry winds

Advances and failures and the exact tone that
eludes us as if losing our sound in an orchestra
unable to simply play G and blend in

But it should be enough it seems to want the
sky-high mirror we can ease through into God's territories
to come down before us or emerge from within us
against the cries of darkest night or its

umbrella-like billows that unflower all around us
their enormous magnolia petals as we swerve through
as straight as we can on the straightest path possible

to the smokeless section
where total clarity reigns and no one suffers from
a dim outline

and the eyes that meet ours burn through space

and link heart to heart via the optic highway

It should be enough to conceive of it
to achieve it

to think of it
to know it

to hold to it
and not let go of it

and maybe it is

and maybe it is
never enough

or maybe it is

4/4

ON READING A NEW POEM BY JACK GILBERT

Sometimes someone's poem catches fire

and you want to ride a sleek grand horse with
silver saddle and bridle into town at a
fast gallop and proclaim it

But it's usually the private overwhelming that has
taken place our solitary heart suddenly elated

giant pipes from Bach's pipe-organ in
some quaint village in Lintz or Metz that
blasts a complex and perfect music

Still when it happens a kind of human vindication
against all loss and unhappiness takes place
a floodgate opening against our usual
humdrum norm of low-key frustration

Simple words put together in such a deft and
reasonably surprising way it literally
unhinges us and leaves us openly flapping in a

very aromatic wind for a while
and we find when we revisit the poem
it still manages to do so time after time
like the perfect combination of a bank safe
that never fails to fall open to our touch
after delicate clinks and clanks inside

We can be as thankful for these brilliant successes
as the rare cardinal in his red plumage and crest
coming to our humble porch bird feeder so that we

stop everything and become very quiet and watchful
even from inside our living room front window

where the whole world passes by

but the joy of it might alight only suddenly and
momentarily

with the highest expectation of its return

                                                        4/6

FACTS CAN BE BROKEN BUT THE TRUTH REMAINS

Facts can be broken but the truth remains

like water frozen in a water jug when the jug's broken
and out pops the jug interior shiny and smooth as glass

Historical moments coalesce around an icy heart
which melts into clear water from a mountain lake

and the truth emerges as facts collide and
crack all around it

(I'm waiting for an example but no
example comes
I have to take my word for it)

But in the moment of an event the apparent
details might add up then burst into
fragments around the strident core
whose existence can't be denied

Light breaks on the ocean floor

Death drives the same limousine as life

At the end of the day all the details add up
to nothing

God steps out and comes toward us
while all the small idols crush into fragments

cling-holds lost and we're left like an
icy core to be melted in God's love
which does take place though it
may take time to come clear

We can't see the truth sometimes for the forest of facts
they go up treacherous mountains on
narrow roads
the hot sun beating down

Distracted by them nevertheless the truth emerges
putting all its shadows to shame

Houses burn down documents are lost
horses gallop from fiery stables and
out over hills into oblivion
but even loss is only a fact put to
shame when truth irradiates and remains

"*God's love*" has an unfortunate sentimental ring to it
but without it billows don't crest
nor stars continue to beam long after they're dead
nor breaths taken in and released nor eyes blink

(I don't know what this poem is about
any more than you do
but I'm willing to be patient to find out)

as the world crumbles to dust and the light of it
stands taller than any of its structures
abstract or solid

We walk away from disaster dazed wondering where the
good is

or caught in its heavy wreckage
until help comes or fails to come

We can't calculate it it eludes what
adds up and continues to baffle us

No fact has a chance in truth's
greater nuclear blast and fallout

Even death is articulate when the details
perfectly assembled fall into logical fragments

Sometimes disaster strikes a death-blow to
crack self's shell and set truth free

once and for all

                                                               4/11

I WENT DOWN TO THE DINER

"Keep you finger on the pearl"
(said to my wife Malika in the "early days")

La única diferencia entre un loco y yo es que no estoy loco
— *Salvador Dali*

I went down to the diner and there were two or three following me
but I turned to them and snarled and they dispersed

As I passed an owl up in a telephone pole greeted me
like it was something we'd carefully rehearsed

The moon was a sliver in a coal black sky
The street lights amber in the shade

I loped along the sidewalk like a wounded gazelle
and I felt the life inside me begin to fade

There was audible talk I could hear quite clearly
coming from somewhere… I don't know

discussing this and that in high hushed voices
but I heard *"immortality of the soul"*

I looked all around but there was no one there
The streets were as deserted as a tomb

but a window opened up above me in the sky
and showed a kind of celestial private room

and there were spectral figures crowding at the opening to take a look
at I presumed the sad loser down below

so I gave a cheerful greeting and a wave of my hand
and suddenly the whole world was in that window

And I wasn't on dark streets and I wasn't in Philadelphia
and I wasn't in any world I could identify

but as if on crystal marbles each with a strong interior light
in an air so pure you couldn't send in a fly

And I was surrounded by crowds of happily avid beings
and I can't even tell you what they were like

their forms were so lit with incredible wattage
that you couldn't see their shapes for the light

And all whispering in voices like close-up waterfalls
rushing in my ears or in my heart

and it was like out in the country far away from people
and I had no desire to depart

Then it all came into focus *I was dead and in heaven!*
They were thrilled to see me and they sang

But I wasn't sure I was ready to be with them
not having heard heaven's gate open with a clang

"You're not dead yet stupid" one said deliriously sweet

"You're not even alive yet you silly fool

*Open your eyes on something way past this world
to the source of the highest priced jewel*

*The pearl on a sea wave in a blast of rare sunlight
whose luster even outshines the sun*

*Matter's kaleidoscope finally resolving its colored images
and folding them all into one*

*The multiplication of mortality is in itself an illusion
in fact there's no one here at all*

*If you open yourself to the furthest limit
you'll see past the latticework wall*

*Start from where you are and fall into its abyss
and sail down past phenomena to zero*

*Then fall through that too and its echoing emptiness
and enter the space that's so narrow*

*not even a gnat can squeeze through not even the
feeler of an ant tinier than the glisten on an atom's eyeball"*

I did all that in the blink of an eye
and landed back on the street after all

still on my way to the late-night diner
with the same appetite I had before

but the world had transformed into a supernatural place
where everything opened a glitteringly crystalline door

and I went through them like a dead man but
unlike a dead man in fact I wasn't dead

And I could see God in front and behind everything I saw
as if someone had screwed diamond eyes in my head

Did this really take place? That I can't tell you
It just took place naturally as I said it —

It seemed totally real to me at least
I just looked deep into my heart and read it —

None of us is really here on our way to a diner
in the dead of night anxiously feeling followed

We're already there to meet us way on up ahead
in the process of eternally being swallowed

back into our forms in a constantly transfigured state
on our way up one street or another

moved way beyond us by a Force beyond us
in the meeting point of Beloved and Lover

4/15

GHOST POEM

There's a cemetery by the sea
overlooking a small seaport

and they have to be extremely vigilant
because many fishing boats leave the

dock with no captain or crew

4/23

SHELLAC

Shellac is the main ingredient in blood
it keeps it hard and supple

What is best about ice is that it's in the shapes of
small gnomes which fit easily into
cardboard boxes under the bed

A stream bordered with milky white cypress trees
runs past the ruined bakery
the one unused for a thousand years and
underground

People are still moving around down there their
bodies covered in white flour and the scent of
dead tulips

There's a movement that can't be called alive and
can't be called death

Three swift ocelots and a bull terrier could
easily symbolize it if it were in any way
symbolic

But this time the cricket sings from the
top of the tree
and the sun goes down in a cup of
marinara sauce only to reappear later
above the lower lid of the sleeping grenadier

When day finally dawns and spreads fresh sheets over
the streets and its people the earth and its worms
the trees and their sailboats
then the elements make their last minute decisions to be
air earth fire water and little silver marbles we keep
in our cheeks in case of emergency

and everything does in fact emerge from the murk
to state its name and serial number before the
firing squad that turns out to be great-great
grandfathers come back from the dead to
save us from ourselves

But our selves have already lost the war
and await the judgment of a small white candle
in a heavy wind

Not that we've sinned
but that the two black liquids of which we are
only the thinnest of barriers want to mingle in the
worst way

and someplace exists that is none of this
where it is safe to pray

4/27

THE DOLPHIN CHORUS

The dolphin chorus has arrived and they're
ready to sing
they're even taking requests

They accompany their songs with rhythmic
water-slaps and fancy dives

Somewhere on this earth of ours something
astonishingly gorgeous is always happening

Plumes of smoke turn into plumes of feathers

Onyx eggs sit quietly next to garden stones
until they're discovered and then become
even more silent as night falls and day dawns

Bus-brakes screech a high C and perfect harmonies appear from
chattering children running in all directions
more operatically dramatic than dying divas

Light from outside things turns tiny cracks
into cathedral windows

Colts drop from their mothers onto wet prairie grass
and wobble a few steps forward

Smoke drifts upward from a meerschaum pipe out a
professor's office window and inebriates a bird's nest

If we turned our veins inside-out wouldn't we be
trees?

If God sat with us on Saturday by Sunday or Monday
wouldn't we carry on as usual
putting dirty clothes into a machine and
setting the dial?

I want to see rainbows in streambeds
rippling along catching golden glints

Clouds bigger than skyscrapers bend down
to touch us on our lips and tongues

Souls of people as we pass on the streets to
display their oracular flags

Each dust mote is a flying carpet for
something smaller

I think the moon may be a dimple on the
sky's cheek

It's the face of the Prophet Muhammad shining over
wide desert dunes

and every camel is in love with its glow
and the camel drivers nearly topple over in the ecstasy of his love

Having said this changes everything

Now we're in a truer domain than ever

His blessed countenance forever gorgeous

And here we'll stay

4/28

COUPLETS (PUNJABI STYLE)

*For Shaykh Masum and his sweet
murid Ahmad Mirza*

1
The raw onion sat in the sun but didn't cook
Deeper than the soul is the Secret and the Secret is in God's precincts

2
Three windows shut one window open the door ajar
Our senses lie in a lying universe but the closed room is open

3
Red roses all over the bush happy as larks in sun or shade
The master sits in an armchair and barely moves while dispensing wisdom

4
The earth sat in a ball of cotton to smooth its rotations
One word of Truth is enough to smash illusion against walls of illusion

5
Mathematics is mainly to do with the relation of rabbits to mud slides
Who exists outside of time and space IS the Creator of time and space

6
If an adventure begins with a whisper and ends with a shout who's to
    blame?
God never leaves the universe alone for even an inconceivable pause
    between nanoseconds

7
The lion ate his dinner then thought of eating me though I objected
A clear heart enters the Unseen without fear of ever being rejected

8
I knew these couplets should rhyme though snow is not made from thunder
The first glimpse of the world beyond this one brings us into a state of wonder

9
The pain in your arm will go away when you lose your body
Eyesight was never keener than when it looked on God's Face

10
The ice on the mountaintop melted into a hot hacienda full of toreadors
A shaky ninety-year old man with a cane may be the fastest runner on the road to God

11
Three flamingoes and a hopscotch diagram make a quizzical conundrum
But a clear drop from the Lake of Love clarifies the whole bodily system in a flash

12
The disappearance of the universe was not something to be scoffed at
though a wise cricket may enlighten the entire garden

13
Into rhyme out of rhyme harmony never entirely eludes us
Three eggs on a somersault tried desperately to keep from cracking

14

Think for a moment of all the places you've never been and how they
    outnumber the places you've been
God's still center has the advantage of being everywhere at once

                                                                           5/3

ONE LINE POEM

Life: you can't talk yourself out of it

5/4

MERCURY POND

If I throw myself into the Mercury Pond will my
eyelashes turn to lead and my tongue to ivory

or the geese within suddenly fly without in
alphabetic formation like a flag unfurling across

fathomless black sky?

The sound here on earth is very quiet

The stars are the only audible elements in this landscape
and they're wailing pathetically across their light years

as if dying of thirst or for their light to stop
traveling through time and space to emerge suddenly from our

deep hearts in full splendor

If I sit still long enough won't I finally die
and the stage set of this world be

struck and fall out into space again from
whence it came?

Or if I sit still long enough I might come to life at last
and debris take on the radiance of sanctified being

eager to harmonize with both distance and nearness
expansion and contraction as its tiny wheels spin

both forward and backward and God

hushes the world with one fall of His Hand
across the sun

5/6

THE FORTY-FOUR EMERALD EARRINGS OF MADAME CHANG

The forty-four emerald earrings of Madame Chang
were mistaken for beetles and
put in a wooden cage

The long waxed mustaches of the prison guard
were mistaken for a broad smile when in fact they were
whips that smote the slightest infraction

The hillside dotted with white stones was mistaken for
sheep though at dusk they didn't seem to
wander in for the night and the nearsighted
shepherd grew dizzy with despair

The long road between walls of tumultuous breakers is mistaken for
a grueling trudge on sore feet
when in fact it's the miracle of Moses opening up a
way through the Red Sea to the Promised Land

and our walk or saunter or lope or dash on it
to the beckoning shore on the other side
can't be mistaken for anything but the sweet
effort of limbs to obey the loving metronome of the
message-bearing heart

And if we're mistaken by half our choices and
decisions and the department store window isn't filled with bargains at all
and the gamble each second presents us with as we
seem to peer forward into the unknown future like

squinting astronomers doesn't always fall to our favor
and all the other Kiplingesque "If's" we can think of

then our contentment with things as they are
*(knowing full well they're projections across eons of the same magic
images that dazzled the denizens of Genghis Khan)*

is the key to see through their frizziling patterns to the
undistorted Pattern-Maker and His Benevolent
intention each moment in so inundating us with all these
bewildering screens

The earrings catching the light on Madame Chang's
earlobes as she sips green tea at noon
the mustaches half-smiling half-growling
announcing themselves by the look on the
prison-guard's face even in a half-light

and the fleecy white rocks on the hillside moseying home after all
where they wait outside the sheepfold gate
to be let in for the night under the

full moon where its full light shines off their
adamant surfaces to glitter like precious gems
and the shepherd is delighted with what he sees
though he sees it fuzzily

and sleeps easy until dawn

THE MATTER AT HAND

A maroon light tunneling forward through a dark gray oval
wall of fuchsias gone dull in smoke

A spatter of spangly disaster-area sparklers
on a rooftop of the Great Pyramid at Giza Hotel

Samson putting all his weight against a temple pillar
as a general darkness blankets the earth like night

"My God what have you done?" to a child found alone with
bloody scissors at the edge of a tangly wood

Three bantam roosters on a fence post waiting for God's
first light to penetrate the sky sitting like a
black coal on a hill of lost souls

Thunderous murderousness in all our hearts
transformed into radiant lace by one drop of Mercy landing on
their hot griddles in back alley soup kitchens

The train leaves the station at exactly two o'clock
as the duchess dies of old age in her cabin
while her lady-in-waiting drowses

The whole earth is peopled by admirable anthropoids
some docile some furious at the ravages of time
though it changes nothing and time marches on

I've shopped at this store before and bought

three gnomes and a tiny kangaroo trapped in amber
though that was years ago before the flood

Language that doesn't urge us toward Allah every second
languishes with the buzzing of flies on a hot day
above puddles of piss

Green light flashing over a meadow in the shapes of
galloping centaurs chasing each other in
play down to a grove of frosted periwinkles

Everything is an altitude and attitude of light
over meadows streams ponds earth-rifts quakes cracks drops
chutes catastrophes and crashes

I hear the clock strike three in the clock tower of my heart
and the town square there fill with gaggles of grounded swans

A little blond girl with one eye closed asks the time from a
gentle grizzly bear who was about to eat her

This could go on or stop though far from here somewhere
black surf under moonlight is getting silver highlights of
foam

God doesn't ponder us
we ponder God

Seeing us
He works directly on the matter at hand

5/13

LATE-NIGHT LEXICONS

A cat is not a cathedral
the same way a dwarf is not a drawer

There's moonlight on Monday
but we can't be sure there's Monday
on the moon

A rat would rather rather not
nor rat on one he'd rated rather high

Moose mosey but mice mustn't

A mouse is a house and a house is a mouse
with their interchangeable h's and m's to make up a home

Do not harass the horse
for a horse keeps to its course
and a caress is best

Clear the deck for Ahab!
He won't go into rehab!

The white whale is a mite pale
though a slab of Ahab roped to his side

is just the trick to make Moby slick

5/19

TEN THOUSAND BUFFALO

I don't know why I should be other than
where I am ever on earth
though I have the feeling I should be
rather than where I am that goes with me
wherever I am on earth

We can never love God too much with a
love that wants nothing in return

The two hundred barbers of Zeiderzee snip
with the same scissors and the same
hair falls to the ground

Though each wave on the sea is a new one
never before seen though it crest and disappear again
unseen by mortal eyes it's a new badge glistening in
raw sunlight before it folds back
into the sea again unseen

If I got up now and continued getting up
until I could get up no further though I
strain and yell and refuse to get down again
until that love I seek contain and graze me

God wears no shoes to be so many places at once
in everyone's apprehension or misapprehension
ideas that trickle through the brains of some
and flush and flash again and again through the
hearts of others until that screen of intensest

light is all and only exists above all
before all and after all
yet no one has gone anywhere but where they
are to get this sudden being where they're not

A little lightning please over in the south corner

A breeze that riffles the papers in our hands
to remind us we're alive

Our deaths will replace us

And we'll still be where we're not

Since God is the only One Who's anywhere

(Ten thousand grazing buffalo can't be wrong)

                                                         5/20

LOVE'S PEBBLES THROWN

One day Love came to town to see if he'd
missed anyone

There was a river he swam to refresh himself

New duck hatchlings in a nest under a grassy bank
needed their natural focus reinforced to the motherly
gratitude of their dam

On the way into town he whistled a new tune
and a farmer boy swooned
and three snakes slithered ecstatically into the ground

Colts got love up their nostrils and moist along their flanks
and galloped over hills until the
sun went down

Even little flames in an oven leapt for joy
and made the bread loaves arranged on their shelves
perfectly brown as if reflecting the sun

which was high overhead when Love got to town

Three on a road out of town came sauntering conversely along
one to go to school one to kill himself unbeknownst to
the others and one to return home before sundown

They met love on the road conversely going into town
and only the suicide recognized him by the

intensity of the gleam in his eye as if the
whole arctic tundra was wide open with aurora borealis
curtains of rose-colored lights shaking like dancers
over its glittering ice
and his heart melted at the sight

and he became very quiet inside the others' laughter at
love's jokes and casual gestures along the
roadside including a dead mouse and a
love letter previously thrown so carelessly down

Love left them and went on into town

An anchorite in a cave remembered
the essence of his vows and sang a song

A couple in the hills lay back in wet grass
and inhaled each other's long contented sighs
that had just encompassed heaven's paradisiacal throng

A fox bit down on a chicken leg after a week of
hunger and wept for joy inside loud and long

The day entered the golden tunnel of its afternoon
No stone was left unturned

No grass blade failed to shiver in Love's updraft

and all perfections were as if brought into a
jeweler's room to be reset and polished to a high sheen
as the sun shone

Love in broad daylight from the depths of night's Throne

None of Love's pebbles from its own place on earth

left unthrown

 5/25

DEATH DROVE A RED POTATO

Death drove a red potato through the back screen door

Everyone in the house suddenly sobbed

The way clouds accumulate in certain parts of the
sky to make mountain landscapes of heavenly cotton
that come apart and reform is always a
silent fascination

The way the sky extends past earth's bright blueness into
all directions and after a while through galaxies and
solar systems more numerous than the pores of our skin
is an abiding mystery

I suppose I too would stop to ponder
and wonder and wish I could
wander yonder

Why can't we see to the far edge? Will we
after we die? Is life blinders and death
their sweet removal?

With my wretched eyesight I keep thinking with death
I'll see everything clearly

"The glory that was Greece and the grandeur that was Rome"
peacocks in constellations calling from branch to
branch from star to star

Gold in the hills igniting

The shadowy figures of time moving through molecules

Waterfalls of light everywhere and
estuaries of silver smoke making the shapes we
take as matter

And be able to hear the real singing all earth's
even most heavenly noises block from our
hearing

and float with it wherever it goes
the way planets and other orbs do

After death takes away the veil with its
rhinoceroses drowsing in mud and
wild cockatoos and fiery flares
at death's intersections

This heart was meant for seeing
These eyes for closing

This heart was meant for singing
These lips for stilling

This body singular as it is
was meant for travel
staying nowhere for the night
a single hand span can't cover

Death sat in the middle of a field and
shouted itself hoarse

She wore a blond wig to cover her
deathly pallor

Red shift blue shift black shift gossamer

With each glimmer we get closer

5/26

THOSE ROSE BUSHES OUT BACK

(for Malika on her birthday)

The roses bloom on your birthday each year
because they want to gauge their beauty by your face
which ages the way understanding of abstruse or simple
wisdom gets clearer and more diamond-like

as water flows under suspension bridges from shore to shore

as herons dip down as quick as flame to spike
fish with their needling beaks and
sink them down their throats in a sudden flash

The room I write this in is full of subtle sounds
various tickings creakings and hums
but no sound as great as the great roar
silence makes all around us

engulfing us

Each tick of time forward or outward from a
timeless center has a silent reverberation against our
bodily cliffs as if surf were wearing us down tick by tick

Will our essential nude beings of radiance walk out of our
bodies one day leaving bone and sinew behind
to embrace His light that comes toward us?

Those roses out back in those bushes you tend so

lovingly still wrapped in their delicate petal prepuces
not yet exposed but ticking forward or outward still
to greet you

There seems to be nothing but encounter in this life of ours
no way out of it even lions in cages have to
wonder how they got there and why

The thing is to close down all encounters but One
and from that One radiates the simple solution to every
unique situation rendering the stretch back of every petal
to form sweet arrays of perfect blossoms

Each growth as I write these words pushes the roses
forward and outward in time a little until
they're in full bloom again
eager to see your face again

year after year

                                                          5/28

SLAPHAPPY

Slaphappy the dapper dandy drove directly in front of
the Big Dipper

"How's that possible granddaddy?" asked the small grasshopper

"I knew you'd ask" said the low lark
wrapped in flannel flying through enamel

Lord this is getting clogged clear the deck for a
new direction

We live for these acts
high wire specialists

"Hope it's no hoax" somberly asked the grand
tusked dragonfly darting through amber

"A glitter on a river gives great pleasure"
said the treasured teacher tackling a
dimmer tincture

Heads nor tails can be made at this
juncture
though that's just conjecture

Reach larger and lighter
Launch the smooth gesture

A single closure guides the clothier

though no haberdasher would dare to crash here

God sits on His throne in an empty theater

We are his collective decapitated glimmer

He looks with an Eye that makes
each celestial swimmer a singer

He
Eternally Singular

5/31

IN SLEEP

In sleep we let our bodies sink

to the bottom of the world

5/31

SOPHOCLES UPON A LOWLY PROMONTORY

Sophocles upon a lowly promontory
gazed at shipwrecks before they clashed with
destiny while all their hands on deck still
swabbed or worked the massive ropes sliding from

sea depths into raw sunlight and their captains
swaggered from task to task above the
common toil

He gazed skyward and saw the wheeling witnesses to
tragedies to come stretch black or white wings
shieldingly across the sun

The heart of Sophocles wept long before their widows heard
news of them name by deep-drenched name
and the soul of Sophocles saw their astonished
faces drift slowly down into darkness after the
crack of rafters and masts and the wrenchings of
rigging became eerily silent again among the
blameworthy rocks as the top waters slid together again
over their human wound

As he turned the earth turned with him a notch and he
faced with his whole wind-ripped body another scene
long before it actually unfolded here
in the human sphere

Sophocles or any other seer

The rain falls gently on the world outside my
window as I write this seeing this thinking this
perpendicular event hit and come full circle
though the circle's in earth and heaven joined for the
silent celebrations we attend in love and death

each day of our's and other's lives on earth
entering heaven by going down in death

past our's and every other's birth

                                                          6/3

SANDWICHED IN BETWEEN TWO UNIVERSES

Sandwiched in between two universes
with palm trees going up into the clouds
never to come back

with its running faucets and its stationary runners
and things going all over the place in all
directions at once

presided over by a benign sky that sometimes turns
vicious though not very often

and really by the look of it lobbed out here in
free space some say is also expanding in
all directions at once so that somehow everything of matter
is moving away from everything else of matter so that
really space is being let in between sorry impacted molecules
in such a way that we can all breathe more
easily

This little planet with its lack of wings but its equator and its
opposing poles *(and this isn't meant to signal a bad
ethnic joke)* and its incredible pluck in

continuing to rotate year after year and century after
century having been spun from the beginning by some
force capable as we see throughout the various galaxies
of some pretty hefty heft in the first place
or else we'd have stopped spinning one would have
thought by now as if on a felt game table though we're

not we're on a black nothingness some say teeters on a
turtle's back who's also on a turtle who's standing on a turtle as well
and so on *"all the way down"* though I rather doubt it

This planet with its gas jets and refrigerators
between actually this world and the next
seen and unseen worlds on top of the
complications of just merely existing
without any fuss

Then there's the matter of multiple dimensions
beyond our usual four to some astronomical number
ghost threads twiddling ecstatically between each

So as I said at the start of this poem
"sandwiched in between two universes" and

probably what I should have said rather than
our little sloshy planet full of bad politics and
worse psychology is
"sandwiched in between two universes is
ourselves"

between birth and death carbohydrates and
cholesterol-free either/or love and its myriad
unreliable opposites
and ultimately after all these millennia
between the devil and the deep blue sea as always
and I'll take the deep blue sea any day

He Who is a drowning worth drowning in since we always

come up singing with no barnacles in our
eyes but stars

and our hearts deeper than the ocean depths
themselves

with His benign shadow thrown always
across them into silvery sunlight

6/4

POETICS

My poetry's source is Allah

but its seedbed is sleep

6/4

POEM FOR ROBERT DESNOS

Robert Desnos I've recently become more
interested in you and your poems

I wonder if I reached far enough into my sleep

I could pull you out and we could
sit here and have a nice chat?

6/5

(Robert Desnos *[1900, Paris - 1945, Terezin Internment Camp, as a political prisoner]*, French Surrealist poet known for his sleep-trance poetry dictations. *From Wikipedia*: Susan Griffin relates a story that exemplifies Desnos' surrealist spirit: "One day Desnos and others were taken away from their barracks. The prisoners rode on the back of a flatbed truck; they knew the truck was going to the gas chamber; no one spoke. Soon they arrived and the guards ordered them off the truck. When they began to move toward the gas chamber, suddenly Desnos jumped out of line and grabbed the hand of the woman in front of him. He was animated and he began to read her palm. The forecast was good: a long life, many grandchildren, abundant joy. A person nearby offered his palm to Desnos. Here, too, Desnos foresaw a long life filled with happiness and success. The other prisoners came to life, eagerly thrusting their palms toward Desnos and, in each case, he foresaw long and joyous lives. The guards became visibly disoriented. Minutes before they were on a routine mission the outcome of which seemed inevitable, but now they became tentative in their movements. Desnos was so effective in creating a new reality that the guards were unable to go through with the executions. They ordered the prisoners back onto the truck and took them back to the barracks. Desnos never was executed. Through the power of imagination, he saved his own life and the lives of others.")

ENIGMATIC POEM FOR MY MOTHER

The challenge resounds through the west of the river
and bounces off the canyon walls like bits of

diamond from a cutting wheel chips and
flint-shapes darts and arrowheads

as twenty-three elders face the fiery sunset in their
unanimous silence

Twenty-three's significance being simply the
very number they were which thereafter became
symbolic of this moment no longer than an
eyelash's fall onto a wet cheek or the death of a
squirrel great-great grandfather by finally falling
from its high branch of refuge onto the forest floor
in death's final pattern as delicious as wild berries
snatched from a bush

The challenge only intensifies the sunset lowering into
each elder's eyes and then into their hearts

They see the end of their lives in this place
they see the drive east from the west of the river
into snow-land and boot-mire without

diamond chip arrowheads or flint darts or
differentiation of seasons or what's

permanent and what's passing faster than ten slow

days of following a kill over hill and dale to its
finality of pattern so far to be hoisted back ten
days or more home and a feast against famine
in this hungry year

She appears as the spirit of the place but is
its servant in her brief apparition clad in
berry leaves and bear-scat and down so fine
breezes blow it this way and silvery that in the
dwindling light

She appears to each elder one by one in place of
the setting sun for her jewelry of punched gold
and pearls this far from sea is in itself a
glittery seduction into the
dark essence of their being

and they become young coal-black lynxes and slide into
the coal-black night

and she stands where they were and closes all of her
forty-six eyes on the darkening sight

6/6
(my mother's birthday)

TO SUPPOSE THAT WE'LL LIVE FOREVER

To suppose that we'll live forever
or even beyond the next moment

is the ephemeral grammar of fireflies flickering
against a very dark sky in a yard made of
colors and variety by day homogeneity by night
into the endlessness that surrounds us

A fiery glove falling through the air

A house whose windows have become thick quartz
so that everyone inside imagines themselves undersea

docked in an eternal world that floats endlessly

All the great poems lament our lack of longevity
though in fact like noses through gelatin
we do go on past materiality's ozones and outer zones
in subtle form whose sound is
in one sense the sound fireflies make inaudible to our
ears to accompany their flickering lights

an infinitesimal firefly sigh that to us would be a shout
across from one to another in the dark

6/8

FIVE SHORT MEDITATIONS ON THE VIRGIN MARY

For Abdal-Hakim Murad

1

The Virgin Mary sat on a rock that was not wholly rock
in a world that was not wholly world

in a light that was Light direct
in the echo of a Command that came from God direct

whose womb was now to house a halo more than she could
possibly long for

and which made her fear
and caused her angel messenger to comfort her

as he stood at the door and mentioned how
God had designated her the hallowed hall for His pure breath to
enter

to make a child with no seed but Himself
to show mankind His holy fatherhood over all

within the physical
but without physical union

2

The pen is hardly lifted

The penalty for birth is death

But he who would be born without coitus
would slide out of death without its mortal coil

Would be taken up to God without entering death's womb
as he had entered Mary's womb without birth's usual folderol

She clutched a tree to steady herself
and dates fell to the ground around her

And he spoke to her from herself
to steady her

Rings of tumult sang around her

The Garden's tree was now there to strengthen her
her nearing it part of God's ordained structure

to redeem Adam and Eve's descent to earth
by new prophecy through standing under
the virgin birth-tree's sacred agency

Adam of no visible parents
Eve of no mother but father Adam's rib-side
being both mother and father

now terrestrialized again in Mary's husbandless pregnancy

though all of us are actually children
of much more than our mere mother's earthly sympathy

3

I saw Mary board a bus at Broad and State
her head covered and her face radiant

small and held within herself
careful and preoccupied

a heaven seeming to be wrapped around her
her cheeks red her lips dry her eyes lowered

interior moisture her preferred cloister
the bus passengers sudden ghosts before her

her shoes small and tattered
her hands carrying a book

If any had spoken to her she might have become lost

If she had spoken to anyone
they might have become saved

4

None can be Mother of God but God
nor Father of flesh but God Himself

Jesus begat in light sat in light and was transformed into light
beyond light's shapes of dark and light

his salutation from where he is continues to excite us
just as Mary's humility brings us home
to where impossible things are true
and true things impossible or possible by our own lights

to submit as purely to God's sheer command of: *Be!*
more than enough to be

in Being's age-long mystery

5

In Ephasis is Artemis
with multitudes of breasts
and legend says where Mary went
and where she died and rests

Teets our forms are fed from
virgin light that salves our souls
the two eternal females
through whom our life unrolls

The Virgin ever virginal
in modesty extreme
and Artemis whose many breasts
supply an endless stream

One statue standing among rocks
the other in her cave
whose house of stone is all alone
within the Light we crave

NOTE

Walking in the woods as is my wont in the morning
June 9th 2005 Philadelphia Pennsylvania after strong storms and
all the trees dry now creaking in the heat and humidity
thinking of this poem
thinking of Mary peace be upon her
walking along the trail wondering to myself about the
Sufi Tariqa of the Mariamiyya
I suddenly hear a crack like horrendous thunder seemingly from
far away but look up above me in time to see a
huge bough break from the top of a tall tree with a giant screech and
hurtle down toward me at seemingly supersonic speed
I step aside yelling *"Allah!"* automatically heart thumping
and the heavy branch crash-lands exactly where I
stood a split second before and breaks into four or five
raw pieces cracked and shattered and me shocked and grateful
thanking Allah over and over thanking Him with all my being
my position just under it one split second before happily not there for it to
crash onto me now safe and sound at the side of the trail
I wonder at the force of it as I continue now to wonder
Allah's full and Awful Power exposed to me direct from the
core of the universe as if sky and earth and mortality itself were
opened up in the blink of an eye

and my life actually only a literal hair's breadth away
from death

At the Thursday night Sufi meeting I describe it in detail
to Baji our Pakistani shaykha and first thing she asks is
"What were you thinking just before the bough broke and fell?"
and when I tell her I was thinking of the Virgin Mary
she says without a moment's pause
"Just as Allah protected and saved Mariam
so Mariam protected you
and saved you!"

6/7-6/9/2005

HOLIDAY FROM THE PERFECT CRIME

All references to north or south or any of the
other myriad divergent directions

All references to crystal doorknobs or the cute
cleft under our noses on our upper lips

Every reference to brands under or over the counter
and all references to persons living or dead

all these things should be ignored in favor of

the slippery essence of the rock-climbing salmon
eyes as wide as heaven itself

or the twinkly bat who hangs upside-down in
dank caves with a few million others squeaking or sleeping

and cubs of any kind from lynxes to wolverines
fumbling over too-big paws and chasing too-thick tails

All these things should be focused on in large measure
as these poems parade past in hopefully the
latest fashions though some may try to appear
naked even more naked than they were
conceived

one by uncertain one on the poetical runway
making their little cool faces or trying to look neutral

or at any moment simply combusting spontaneously
and ending up a shower of multicolored sparks
in shapes of wizards or doppelgängers or your
next door neighbor simply watering her hydrangeas

inhabiting or being inhabited by vibratory
presences and strobe-light interiorizations that
actually push out from within to dictate certain
unmistakable shapes tree shapes sword shapes
word shapes themselves whether or not they
describe or hide

In fact disregard even the actual words themselves
altogether as well as the paper they're printed on or the
airwaves you hear them in

and even the world they appear in disregard
that as well until we're safely in a place where
none of this is taking place and never has and
never will

and there we'll find ourselves perhaps in our
original state before any references or inferences or
conferences or deferences could even be
made

Aunt Virgin Mary of the rocks helping us from her
eternal lookout and

Brother Jesus of the Strong Ray holding out both
hands to us where he always is

and all people in earth and heaven

Muhammad peace be upon him and them all at once

who enters conscious space just once

and is then here forever as our

luminous perfection

6/11

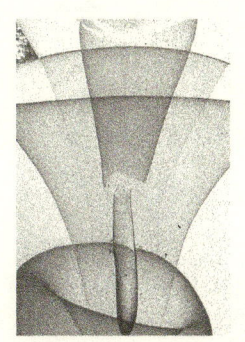

INDEX

A Line All by Itself   16
Couplets (Punjabi Style)   88
Death Drove a Red Potato   104
Each   61
Enigmatic Poem for My Mother   119
Facts Can Be Broken But the Truth Remains   75
First and Last Lion   13
Five Short Meditations on the Virgin Mary   122
Flying Saucers   57
Ghost Poem   82
Giant Steps   38
Holiday from the Perfect Crime   128
Hotel Delirium   17
I Went Down to the Diner   78
In Sleep   111
It Should Be Enough   71
Late-Night Lexicons   98
Line Left Over From a Dream   66
Lines Written During a Flu   49
Love's Pebbles Thrown   101
Mercury Pond   92
On Reading a New Poem by Jack Gilbert   73
One Line Poem / "Life..."   91
One Line Poem / "One day..."   48
One Line Poem / "The cat..."   53
On the Lip of Sleep   27
Poem for Robert Desnos   118
Poetics   117
Sandwiched in Between Two Universes   114
Savage and Silly   15
Shellac   83
Silence Overtakes Us in the End   39
Slaphappy   109
Sophocles Upon a Lowly Promontory   112
Stauffer Makes a Long Landing   23
Takeeti Tapeeti   54

Ten Thousand Buffalo   99
The Blues   35
The Boy Who Sought to Put Death to Death   50
The Bullet   29
The Dolphin Chorus   85
The Forty-Four Emerald Earrings of Madame Chang   94
The Glimpse   19
The Key Motivation   59
The Lover The Beloved   69
The Matter at Hand   96
The Narrative   32
The Non-Existent Noble Arch   63
The Sin of the Shoe   21
The Sumptuous Honey of Words   67
The Surgeon   36
The Wild Red Rooster   43
Those Rose Bushes Out Back   107
To Maintain the Proper Temperature   25
To Suppose That We'll Live Forever   121
Trilogy   45
Where Feet are Superfluous   11
Zog The Speechless Anthracite   42

ABOUT THE AUTHOR

Born in 1940 in Oakland, California, Daniel Abdal-Hayy Moore's first book of poems, *Dawn Visions*, was published by Lawrence Ferlinghetti of City Lights Books, San Francisco, in 1964, and the second in 1972, *Burnt Heart/Ode to the War Dead*. He created and directed *The Floating Lotus Magic Opera Company* in Berkeley, California in the late 60s, and presented two major productions, *The Walls Are Running Blood*, and *Bliss Apocalypse*. He became a Sufi Muslim in 1970, performed the Hajj in 1972, and lived and traveled throughout Morocco, Spain, Algeria and Nigeria, landing in California and publishing *The Desert is the Only Way Out*, and *Chronicles of Akhira* in the early 80s (Zilzal Press). Residing in Philadelphia since 1990, in 1996 he published *The Ramadan Sonnets* (Jusoor/City Lights), and in 2002, *The Blind Beekeeper* (Jusoor/Syracuse University Press). He has been the major editor for a number of works, including *The Burdah* of Shaykh Busiri, translated by Shaykh Hamza Yusuf, and the poetry of Palestinian poet, Mahmoud Darwish, translated by Munir Akash. He is also widely published on the worldwide web: *The American Muslim, DeenPort*, and his own website and poetry blog, among others: *www.danielmoorepoetry.com*, *www.ecstaticxchange.wordpress.com*. He has been poetry editor for *Islamica Magazine*, and *Seasons Journal*, a new translation by Munir Akash of *State of Siege*, by Mahmoud Darwish, from Syracuse University Press, and *The Prayer of the Oppressed* of Imam Nasir al-Dar'i, translated by Hamza Yusuf. The Ecstatic Exchange Series is bringing out the extensive body of his works of poetry (a complete list of published works on page 2).

POETIC WORKS by Daniel Abdal-Hayy Moore
Published and Unpublished

Dawn Visions (published by City Lights, 1964)
Burnt Heart/Ode to the War Dead (published by City Lights, 1972)
This Body of Black Light Gone Through the Diamond (printed by Fred Stone, Cambridge, Mass, 1965)
On The Streets at Night Alone (1965?)
All Hail the Surgical Lamp (1967)
States of Amazement (1970)

Abdallah Jones and the Disappearing-Dust Caper (published by The Ecstatic Exchange/Crescent Series, 2006)
'Ala ud-Deen and the Magic Lamp
The Chronicles of Akhira (1981) (published by Zilzal Press with Typoglyphs by Karl Kempton, 1986)(published in Sparrow on the Prophet's Tomb by The Ecstatic Exchange, 2009)
Mouloud (1984) (A Zilzal Press chapbook, 1995)(published in Sparrow on the Prophet's Tomb by The Ecstatic Exchange, 2009)
Man is the Crown of Creation (1984)
The Look of the Lion (The Parabolas of Sight) (1984)
The Desert is the Only Way Out (completed 4/21/84) (Zilzal Press chapbook, 1985)
Atomic Dance (1984) (am here books, 1988)
Outlandish Tales (1984)
Awake as Never Before (12/26/84) (Zilzal Press chapbook, 1993)
Glorious Intervals (1/1/85) (Zilzal Press chapbook, ?)
Long Days on Earth/Book I (1/28 – 8/30/85)
Long Days on Earth/Book II (Hayy Ibn Yaqzan)
Long Days on Earth/Book III (1/22/86)
Long Days on Earth/Book IV (1986)
The Ramadan Sonnets (Long Days on Earth/Book V) (5/9 – 6/11/86) (published by Jusoor/City Lights Books, 1996) (republished as Ramadan Sonnets by The Ecstatic Exchange, 2005)
Long Days on Earth/Book VI (6-8/30/86)
Holograms (9/4/86 – 3/26/87)
History of the World (The Epic of Man's Survival) (4/7 – 6/18/87)

Exploratory Odes (6/25 – 10/18/87)
The Man at the End of the World (11/11 – 12/10/87)
The Perfect Orchestra (3/30 – 7/25/88) (published by The Ecstatic Exchange, 2009)
Fed from Underground Springs (7/30 – 11/23/88)
Ideas of the Heart (11/27/88 – 5/5/89)
New Poems (scattered poems, out of series, from 3/24 – 8/9/89)
Facing Mecca (5/16 – 11/11/89)
A Maddening Disregard for the Passage of Time (11/17/89 – 5/20/90) (published by The Ecstatic Exchange, 2009)
The Heart Falls in Love with Visions of Perfection (6/15/90 – 6/2/91)
Like When You Wave at a Train and the Train Hoots Back at You (Farid's Book) (6/11 – 7/26/91) (published by The Ecstatic Exchange, 2008)
Orpheus Meets Morpheus (8/1/91 – 3/14/92)
The Puzzle (3/21/92 – 8/17/93)
The Greater Vehicle (10/17/93 – 4/30/94)
A Hundred Little 3-D Pictures (5/14/94 – 9/11/95)
The Angel Broadcast (9/29 – 12/17/95)
Mecca/Medina Time-Warp (12/19/95 – 1/6/96) (published as a Zilzal Press chapbook, 1996)(published in Sparrow on the Prophet's Tomb by The Ecstatic Exchange, 2009)
Miracle Songs for the Millennium (1/20 – 10/16/96)
The Blind Beekeeper (11/15/96 – 5/30/97) (published 2002 by Jusoor/Syracuse University Press)
Chants for the Beauty Feast (6/3 – 10/28/97)(published by The Ecstatic Exchange, 2011)
You Open a Door and it's a Starry Night (10/29/97 – 5/23/98) (published by The Ecstatic Exchange, 2009)
Salt Prayers (5/29 – 10/24/98) (published by The Ecstatic Exchange, 2005)
Some (10/25/98 – 4/25/99)
Flight to Egypt (5/1 – 5/16/99)
I Imagine a Lion (5/21 – 11/15/99) (published by The Ecstatic Exchange, 2006)
Millennial Prognostications (11/25/99 – 2/2/2000) (published by the Ecstatic Exchange, 2009)
Shaking the Quicksilver Pool (2/4 – 10/8/2000) (published by The Ecstatic Exchange, 2009)
Blood Songs (10/9/2000 – 4/3/2001)
The Music Space (4/10 – 9/16/2001) (published by The Ecstatic Exchange, 2007)

Where Death Goes (9/20/2001 – 5/1/2002) (published by The Ecstatic Exchange, 2009)
The Flame of Transformation Turns to Light (99 Ghazals Written in English) (5/14 – 8/21/2002) (published by The Ecstatic Exchange, 2007)
Through Rose-Colored Glasses (7/22/2002 – 1/15/2003) (published by The Ecstatic Exchange, 2007)
Psalms for the Broken-Hearted (1/22 – 5/25/2003) (published by The Ecstatic Exchange, 2006)
Hoopoe's Argument (5/27 – 9/18/03)
Love is a Letter Burning in a High Wind (9/21 – 11/6/2003) (published by The Ecstatic Exchange, 2006)
Laughing Buddha/Weeping Sufi (11/7/2003 – 1/10/2004) (published by The Ecstatic Exchange, 2005)
Mars and Beyond (1/20 – 3/29/2004) (published by The Ecstatic Exchange, 2005)
Underwater Galaxies (4/5 – 7/21/2004) (published by The Ecstatic Exchange, 2007)
Cooked Oranges (7/23/2004 – 1/24/2005 (published by The Ecstatic Exchange, 2007)
Holiday from the Perfect Crime (1/25 – 6/11/2005)(published by The Ecstatic Exchange, 2011)
Stories Too Fiery to Sing Too Watery to Whisper (6/13 – 10/24/2005)
Coattails of the Saint (10/26/2005 – 5/10/2006) (published by The Ecstatic Exchange, 2006)
In the Realm of Neither (5/14 – 11/12/06) (published by The Ecstatic Exchange, 2008)
Invention of the Wheel (11/13/06 – 6/10/07) (published by The Ecstatic Exchange, 2010)
The Sound of Geese Over the House (6/15 – 11/4/07)
The Fire Eater's Lunchbreak (11/11/07 – 5/19/2008) (published by The Ecstatic Exchange, 2008)
Sparks Off the Main Strike (5/24/2008 – 1/10/2009) (published by The Ecstatic Excange, 2010)
Stretched Out on Amethysts (1/13 – 9/17/2009) (published by The Ecstatic Exchange, 2010)
The Throne Perpendicular to All that is Horizontal (9/18/09 – 1/25/10)
In Constant Incandescence (2/10 – 8/13/10) (published by The Ecstatic Exchange, 2011)
The Caged Bear Spies the Angel (8/30/10 – 3/6/11)
This Light Slants Upward (3/7/11 --)

www.ingramcontent.com/pod-product-compliance
Lightning Source LLC
Chambersburg PA
CBHW020910090426
42736CB00008B/568